Edward E. Bowen

Harrow Songs

And other Verses

Edward E. Bowen

Harrow Songs
And other Verses

ISBN/EAN: 9783744772198

Printed in Europe, USA, Canada, Australia, Japan

Cover: Foto ©Thomas Meinert / pixelio.de

More available books at **www.hansebooks.com**

HARROW SONGS

AND OTHER VERSES

BY

EDWARD E. BOWEN

LONDON
LONGMANS, GREEN, AND CO.
1886

All rights reserved

LOAN STACK

THE songs which are here reprinted were written at various times during the last eighteen years, and have found an indulgent reception at the hands of several generations of schoolboys. For whatever interest they may have awakened, they are chiefly indebted to the genius and skill of Mr. John Farmer, by whom nearly all of them have been set to music, and presented to an audience which, for the sake of the singers, as well as for his, has never been too harshly critical of the sentiments or the words. I ought to mention that some of the lines in No. XV., and two or three in No. XVIII., are the work of a friend.

A few other pieces are added, chiefly connected with Harrow; these, though not of permanent interest, will perhaps find readers who may care to have them in print.

[The words and music of most of the songs may be had from Mr. Wilbee, of Harrow.]

CONTENTS.

		PAGE
I.	FORTY YEARS ON	1
II.	LYON OF PRESTON	3
III.	RALEIGH	5
IV.	QUEEN ELIZABETH	7
V.	ST. JOLES	10
VI.	SHE WAS A SHEPHERDESS	13
VII.	GRANDPAPA'S GRANDPAPA	15
VIII.	'BYRON LAY'	17
IX.	GIANTS	19
X.	OCTOBER	22
XI.	EUCLID	24
XII.	THE VOICE OF THE BELL	27
XIII.	UNDERNEATH THE BRINY SEA	29
XIV.	SOBER DICK	32
XV.	WILLOW THE KING	35
XVI.	JUNE AND THE SCHOLAR	38

		PAGE
XVII. CATS AND DOGS	.	40
XVIII. FAIRIES	.	42
XIX. JACK AND JOE	.	45
XX. WIMBLEDON, 1879	.	48
XXI. LARRY	.	50
XXII. ROOKS	.	52
XXIII. DOWN THE HILL	.	54
XXIV. AWAKE	.	56
XXV. GOOD NIGHT	.	58
XXVI. SONGS	.	60

LORD'S, 1873	63
LORD'S, 1878	66
BUTTERMERE INN, CRUMMOCKWATER	68
AN EPISODE OF BALACLAVA	71
P. L. C.	74
SHEMUEL	76
R. G.	78

I

FORTY YEARS ON

FORTY years on, when afar and asunder
    Parted are those who are singing to-day,
When you look back, and forgetfully wonder
    What you were like in your work and your play;
Then, it may be, there will often come o'er you
    Glimpses of notes like the catch of a song—
Visions of boyhood shall float them before you,
    Echoes of dreamland shall bear them along.
        Follow up! Follow up! Follow up! Follow up!
           Till the field ring again and again,
        With the tramp of the twenty-two men,
           Follow up! Follow up!

Routs and discomfitures, rushes and rallies,
    Bases attempted, and rescued, and won,
Strife without anger, and art without malice,—
    How will it seem to you, forty years on?
Then, you will say, not a feverish minute
    Strained the weak heart and the wavering knee,
Never the battle raged hottest, but in it
    Neither the last nor the faintest were we!
        Follow up! &c.

O the great days, in the distance enchanted,
    Days of fresh air, in the rain and the sun,
How we rejoiced as we struggled and panted—
    Hardly believable, forty years on !
How we discoursed of them, one with another,
    Auguring triumph, or balancing fate,
Loved the ally with the heart of a brother,
    Hated the foe with a playing at hate !
        Follow up ! &c.

Forty years on, growing older and older,
    Shorter in wind, as in memory long,
Feeble of foot, and rheumatic of shoulder,
    What will it help you that once you were strong ?
God give us bases to guard or beleaguer,
    Games to play out, whether earnest or fun ;
Fights for the fearless, and goals for the eager,
    Twenty, and thirty, and forty years on !
        Follow up ! &c.

II

LYON OF PRESTON

LYON, of Preston, yeoman, John,
    Many a year ago,
Built on the hill that I live on,
    A school that you all may know ;
Into the form, first day, 'tis said,
    Two boys came for to see ;
One with a red ribbon, red, red, red,
    And one with a blue,—like me !

Lyon, of Preston, yeoman, John,
    Lessons he bade them do ;
Homer, and multiplica-ti-on,
    And spelling, and Cicero ;
Red Ribbon never his letters knew,
    Stuck at the five times three ;
But Blue Ribbon learnt the table through,
    And said it all off,—like me !

Lyon, of Preston, yeoman, John,
    Said to them both, ' Go play '—
Up slunk Red Ribbon all alone,
    Limped from the field away ;

Blue Ribbon played like a hero's son,
    All by himself played he,
Five 'runs up' did he quickly run,
    And Bases got five,—like me!

Lyon, of Preston, yeoman, John,
    All in his anger sore,
Flogged the boy with the Red ribbon,
    Set him the Georgics four;
But the boy with the Blue ribbon got, each week,
    Holidays two and three,
And a prize for sums, and a prize for Greek,
    And an alphabet prize,—like me!

Lyon, of Preston, yeoman, John,
    Died many years ago;
All that is mortal of him is gone,
    But he lives in a school I know!
All of them work at their football there,
    And work at their five-times-three;
And all of them, ever since that day, wear
    A ribbon of blue,—like me!

III

RALEIGH

WHEN Raleigh rose to fight the foes,
    We sprang to work and will;
When Glory gave to Drake the wave,
    She gave to us the Hill.
The ages drift in rolling tide,
    But high shall float the morn
Adown the stream of England's pride,
    When Drake and we were born!
      For we began when he began,
        Our times are one;
      His glory thus shall circle us
        Till time be done.

The Avon bears to endless years
    A magic voice along,
Where Shakespeare strayed in Stratford's shade,
    And waked the world to song.
We heard the music soft and wild,
    We thrilled to pulses new;
The winds that reared the Avon's child
    Were Herga's nurses too.
      For we began, &c.

Guard, guard it well, where Sidney fell,
    The poet-soldier's grave;
Thy life shall roll, O royal soul,
    In other hearts as brave.
While Thought to wisdom wins the gay,
    While Strength upholds the free,
Are we the sons of yesterday,
    Or heirs of thine and thee?
      For we began, &c.

IV

QUEEN ELIZABETH

QUEEN ELIZABETH sat one day,
    Watching her mariners rich and gay,
And there were the Tilbury guns at play
    And there was the bold sea rover;
Up comes Lyon, so brisk and free,
Makes his bow, and he says, says he,
'Gracious Queen of the land and sea,
    From Tilbury fort to Dover—'
        Queen Elizabeth, &c.

'Marry, come up,' says good Queen Bess,
'Draw it shorter and prose it less;
Speeches are things we chiefly bless
    When once we have got them over;
Spenser carries you well along,
And the Swan of Avon is rich in song—
Still, we have sometimes found them long,
    I and the bold sea rover!'
        Queen Elizabeth, &c.

'Queen,' he says, 'I have got in store,
A beautiful school from roof to door;
And I have a farm of acres four,
 And a meadow of grass and clover:
So may it please you, good Queen B.,
Give me a charter, firm and free;
For there is Harrow, and this is me,
 And that is the bold sea rover!'
  Queen Elizabeth, &c.

'Bad little boys,' says she, 'at school
Want a teacher to rede and rule;
Train a dunce, and you find a fool;
 Cattle must have their drover:
By my halidome, I propose
You be teacher of verse and prose—
(What's a halidome, no one knows,
 Even the bold sea rover!)'
  Queen Elizabeth, &c.

'And this is my charter, firm and free,
This is my royal, great decree—
Hits to the rail shall count for three,
 And six when fairly over:

And if any one comes and makes a fuss,
Send the radical off to us,
And I will tell him I choose it thus,
   And so will the bold sea rover!'
    Queen Elizabeth, &c.

V

ST. JOLES

WHEN time was young and the school was new,
(King James had painted it bright and blue),
In sport or study, in grief or joy,
St. Joles was the friend of the lazy boy.
He helped when the lesson at noon was said,
He helped when the Bishop was fast in bed;
For the Bishop of course was master then,
And bishops get up at the stroke of ten.
   St. Joles hooray, and St. Joles hooroo,
   Mark my word if it don't come true;
   In sport or study, in grief or joy,
   St. Joles is the friend of the lazy boy.

If an *a* was possibly short or long,
St. Joles would whisper it right (or wrong);
If ever an *e* provoked a doubt,
St. Joles' Lexicon helped it out;
Perhaps it wasn't in page and print,
But it hinted a probable friendly hint;

And often indeed, if I must confess,
It was like to a sort of a kind of guess.
      St. Joles hooray, &c.

No laws of scholarship, harsh and quaint,
Could ever perplex the useful Saint;
No trouble of mood or gender come,
But he settled the rule by the rule of thumb;
You could toss a penny, and surely know
The way the genitive case would go;
For at tails and heads he was clear and true,
And it always turned up one of the two!
      St. Joles hooray, &c.

But there came a morning of fear and dread,
When the Bishop was up, and the Saint in bed;
And all the boys, from bottom to top,
Instead of bishop, pronounced bishóp!—
—However the guilty class might try,
They lengthened *o* and they shortened *i*;
And the Bishop with righteous anger flames;
And off he went, and he told King James.
      St. Joles hooray, &c.

O then King James, in his wrath and ire,
Degraded St. Joles to Joles Esquire;
And now, to punish the awful crime,
They get up at seven in winter time;

And oft the vowels in prose and song
St. Joles' Lexicon tells you wrong;
And if you believe me, down at play,
There's always fog on St. Joles' day.
  St. Joles hooray, &c.

VI

SHE WAS A SHEPHERDESS

SHE was a Shepherdess, O so fair,
    Many a year ago,
With a pail and a stool and tangled hair,
    Down in the plain below;
And all the scholars would leave their play,
On merry King Charles's own birthday,
And stand and look as she passed that way,
    And see her a-milking go;
      But none, she said,
      Will I ever wed,
But the boy who gets the Gregory prize,
And crosses his *t*'s and dots his *i*'s,
    Down in the plain below.

Sorely the monitor, great in Greek,
    Many a year ago,
And the cricketing captain, slim and sleek,
    Down in the plain below;

Sorely the Latiner daily tried,
With satchel and ciphering books at side,
To make her his beautiful blooming bride,
  As he saw her a-milking go !
   But none, &c.

So the Gregory prizeman won the maid,
  Many a year ago,
And the bells were rung and the service said,
  Down in the plain below ;
And the cows gave double their milk that day,
And merry King Charles came down to stay,
And the fags had a general hip hooray,
  As they saw her a-milking go.
   But none, &c.

And if this ditty of love be true,
  Many a year ago,
(And you'll please forgive our singing it you)
  Down in the plain below ;
O was there ever so sweet a pair,
As both of them went a-milking there,
With a pail and a stool and tangled hair,
  A milking for to go.
   But none, &c.

VII

GRANDPAPA'S GRANDPAPA

DO you know, grandpapa's grandpapa
    Had of study so unquenchable a thirst,
That he went off to Harrow, fa la la !
    And was placed in Lower Lower First.
How the buttons on his blue frock shone !
    How he carolled and he sang, like a bird !
And Rodney, the sailor boy, was one,
    And Bruce, who travelled far, was the third.
        For you know, &c.

Then to Bruce grandpapa's grandpapa
    Said, ' Bruce ' (who travelled far) ' come along,
We are ten summers old, fa la la !
    So to hoops, and to merriment, and song !'
' Oh no ! though I mourn,' he said, ' in truth,
    G's G., merry rollicking to mar,
What's hoops, and effusiveness of youth,
    To a lad who has got to travel far ! '
        For you know, &c.

Then to Rodney grandpapa's grandpapa
    Said, ' Rodney, sailor boy, up away !
And with marbles, and with tops, fa la la !
    'Mid the merry folks from town, pass the day.'
But Rodney, sailor boy, ' No,' said he,
    ' Brace tackles, and avast, and alas !
No marbles and jollity for me ;
    I have got to beat the French and de Grasse ! '
        For you know, &c.

Then, then, grandpapa's grandpapa
    Went revelling away, in and out,
'Mid the merry folks from town, fa la la !
    While the marbles and the tops flew about.
And of all the merry folks, fa la la !
    In buttons and in blue frocks drest,
Why be sure, grandpapa's grandpapa
    Was the topmost and merriest and best !
        For you know, &c.

VIII

'BYRON LAY'

BYRON lay, lazily lay,
   Hid from lesson and game away,
  Dreaming poetry, all alone,
  Up-a-top of the Peachey stone.
All in a fury enters Drury,
  Sets him grammar and Virgil due ;
Poets shouldn't have, shouldn't have, shouldn't have,
  Poets shouldn't have work to do.

  Peel stood, steadily stood,
    Just by the name in the carven wood,
   Reading rapidly, all at ease,
   Pages out of Demosthenes.
' Where has he got to ? Tell him not to ! '
  All the scholars who hear him, cry,
' That's the lesson for, lesson for, lesson for,
  That's the lesson for next July ! '

   Peel could never, you needs must own,
    Rhyme one rhyme on the Peachey stone ;
    Byron never his task have said,
    Under the panel where PEEL is read.

'Even a goose's brain has uses'—
　　Cricketing comrades argued thus—
'Will they ever be, ever be, ever be,
　　Will they ever be boys like us?'

　　　Byron lay, solemnly lay,
　　　Dying for freedom, far away:
　　　Peel stood up on the famous floor,
　　　Ruled the people, and fed the poor;
None so narrow the range of Harrow;
　　Welcome poet and statesman too;
Doer and dreamer, dreamer, dreamer,
　　Doer and dreamer, dream and do!

IX

GIANTS

THERE were wonderful giants of old, you know,
    There were wonderful giants of old;
They grew more mightily, all of a row,
    Than ever was heard or told;
All of them stood their six feet four,
And they threw to a hundred yards or more,
And never were lame, or stiff, or sore;
And we, compared with the days of yore,
    Are cast in a pigmy mould.
        For all of we,
        Whoever we be,
Come short of the giants of old, you see.

There were splendid cricketers then, you know,
    There were splendid cricketers then;
The littlest drove for a mile or so,
    And the tallest drove for ten:
With Lang to bowl and Hankey to play,
Webbe and Walker to score and stay—

And two that I know, but may not say,—
But we are a pitiful race of clay,
   And never will score again.
      For all of we,
       Whoever we be,
   Come short of the giants of old, you see.

There were scholars of marvellous force, you know,
   There were scholars of marvellous force;
They never put μὴ when they should put οὐ,
   And the circle they squared, of course.
With Blayds and Merivale, Hope, Monro,
Ridley and Hawkins, years ago,—
And one that I rather think I know—
But we are heavy and dull and slow,
   And growing duller and worse;
      For all of we,
       Whoever we be,
   Come short of the giants of old, you see.

But I think all this is a lie, you know,
   I think all this is a lie;
For the hero-race may come and go,
   But it doesn't exactly die!
For the match we lose and win it again,
And a Balliol comes to us now and then,

And if we are dwarfing in bat and pen,
Down to the last of the Harrow men,
  We will know the reason why!
      For all of we,
      Whoever we be,
Come up to the giants of old, you see.

X

OCTOBER

THE months are met, with their crownlets on,
    As Julius Cæsar crowned them;
With slaves, the gentlemen thirty-one,
    And the ladies thirty, round them.
But who shall be monarch of all, you ask;
    Go ask of the boys and maidens,
For that is the lads' and the lasses' task,
    And they choose him afar in cadence.
        October! October!
        March to the dull and sober!
      The suns of May for the schoolgirls' play,
        But give to the boys October!

'*I vote for March, may it please you,*' cries
    A student pale and meagre;
'*He gives us theme and lesson and prize,*
    And scholarship, O so eager!'
But louder now in the distance floats
    A choice there is no disguising;
And you hear from two and twenty throats
    The chaunt of the boys uprising.
        October! &c.

'*For May! For May!*' the girls all say,
  '*How mild the air that blows is!*
How nicely sweet the soft spring day,
  How sweetly nice the roses!'
But girl and scholar may pray and plead—
  The voice of the lads is clearer,
And forty and four are the feet that tread,
  In time to the music, nearer!
    October! &c.

' October brings the cold weather down,
  When the wind and the rain continue;
He nerves the limbs that are lazy grown,
  And braces the languid sinew;
So while we have voices and lungs to cheer,
  And the winter frost before us,
Come sing to the king of the mortal year,
  And thunder him out in chorus!'
    October! October!
    March to the dull and sober!
    The suns of May for the schoolgirls' play,
    But give to the boys October!

XI

EUCLID

O HAVE you, with Euclid before you,
    Full often despairingly sat,
The Fifth Proposition to floor you,
    Your mind getting blank as your hat?
To the little black demon you owe it,
    The corner at C is his den;
He waits till you fancy you know it,
    Then makes you forget it again.
        For he sits, a sight for to dream on,
            In his black boots, tall and thin;
        And some people call him a demon,
            And others a hobgoblin.

O worse than the rock to the seaman,
    O worse than the blight to the tree,
Is the face of the little black demon,
    Who lives in the corner at C.
He hops and he jumps without reason
    All over and under and through,
And grins as he teaches his treason
    To logic, and Euclid, and you.
        For he sits, &c.

How sides, by a curious juggle,
    Together are less than the base ;
How parallel lines, with a struggle,
    Succeed in enclosing a space ;
Then mixing up angle and angle,
    Puts lines where no line ought to be,
And leaving your mind in a tangle,
    Goes back to his corner at C.
        For he sits, &c.

But I up and I went and I took him,
    All capering under and o'er,
And didn't he cry as I shook him,
    And didn't I shake him the more,
And taught him respect for his betters,
    And thumped on his black little head,
And squeezed him the shape of all letters,
    And finally left him at Z !
        For he sits, &c.

And often as, nightly or daily,
    He dares to annoy you the least,
You have only to rush at him gaily,
    Away goes the black little beast ;

> And all the bad creatures forsaken,
> That live on the page or the pen,
> Can't bear to be worried and shaken,
> And run away home to their den,
> For he sits, &c.

XII

THE VOICE OF THE BELL

EVERY day, in the early misty morning,
    Hark how the bell is ringing, ding-a-ding, ding:
First for a waking, second for a warning,
    Hark how the bell is ringing, ding-a-ding, ding:
  Oh, what a tongue to terrify the lazy,
  Never a respite, never stops or stays he,
  On till the ears of the listeners are crazy,
    Ding, ding-a-ding!

Down at the game, a wearying and bruising,
    Hark how the bell is ringing, ding-a-ding, ding:
Comes now a truce to winning and to losing,
    Hark how the bell is ringing, ding-a-ding, ding.
  Then, though the hill be muddy and begriming,
  Victory yet can make it easy climbing:
  Bless the bell, for the triumph it is chiming!
    Ding, ding-a-ding.

Half-past five, in the gloomy winter weather,
    Hark how the bell is ringing, ding-a-ding, ding ;
Now to the fireside gather you together,
    Hark how the bell is ringing, ding-a-ding, ding.
Safe from the thought of boy or book or master,
Fourth school's bliss—or possible disaster—
Wish that the weeks might fly a little faster,
    Ding, ding-a-ding.

Long long life to the bell and to its ringing !
    Hark how the bell is ringing, ding-a-ding, ding :
Three hundred years with an ever fresh beginning !
    Hark how the bell is ringing, ding-a-ding, ding ;
Long while it chimes to a newer life and sweeter,
Work's true sons shall welcome her and greet her,
Stronger than we, and better, and completer,
    Ding, ding, ding.

XIII

UNDERNEATH THE BRINY SEA

UNDERNEATH the briny sea,
    Where be the fishes and the mermaids three,
There lies Harrow as it ought for to be !
Big fish and little there, each shiny day,
Climb up to construe, plunge down to play ;
Get wise speedily, up upon the hill,
Coming up to all schools just when they will ;
Play well easily, weed and sand among,
Never lose a match there, all the summer long ;
Never take to bad ways, bully, steal, or lie,
Fishes all are born good, naturally !
    Underneath the briny sea,
    Where be the fishes and the mermaids three,
    There lies Harrow as it ought for to be !

Bills when the fishes like, lock up as they wish,
Bolts and bars confine not independent fish ;
Fruit sells for nothing there, if you like to buy,
Ices all the year long tumble from the sky !

No trouble anywhere, labour none at all,
Twenty scores of fags come rushing when you call;
Twenty scores of fags come, never miss it—why?
Fagging does itself all by machinery!
    Underneath the briny sea,
    Where be the fishes and the mermaids three,
    There lies Harrow as it ought for to be!

Oh, what a life there, down below the wave,
All among the sand heaps, merry fishes have!
Lessons get the full mark, whether bad or good,
Fishes never guess wrong—couldn't if they would;
Greek turns to English by the rule of thumb;
Sums have the answer written on the sum;
Repetition learns itself, never need to try—
Everyone has prizes, generally.
    Underneath the briny sea,
    Where be the fishes and the mermaids three,
    There lies Harrow as it ought for to be!

Which is the better, man, or boy, or fish,
To live life lazily, swimming as you wish,
Lolling dull heads about, twirling weary thumbs,
Or to take sweet and bitter as sweet and bitter comes?
Wealth without toil is a sorry sort of lot;
Learning unworked for is just as well forgot;

Good beats bad, when the fight is only free,
Both up at Harrow here, and under the sea.
   Underneath the briny sea,
    Where be the fishes and the mermaids three,
   There lies Harrow as it ought for to be!

XIV

SOBER DICK

WHAT sober Dicky sees,
 When all aglow
Fire lights the winter nights,
 Boys only know.
Out, gas—no soul it has—
 Out lamp and wick;
In the embers, ruddily gilt,
Wonderful things are often built;
Sober Dicky can see them all, O sober Dick!

There lies a field of grass,
 Ropes all around;
Who's that has got the bat,
 Hits off the ground?
Who plays amid the blaze,
 All ruby-thick?
Coals applaud with a coaly cry,
Sparks in yellow and amber fly;
Sober Dicky it surely is, O sober Dick!

See, in the stately light
    Glows yonder Hall;
Folks sent to Parliament,
    Pitt, Fox, and all.
One big amazing wig
    Flares hot and quick;
Mr. Speaker is made of coal,
Yet you will think it wondrous droll,
Like to sober Dicky he is, O sober Dick!

Where, chin on hand, he looks
    Right through the bars,
Yon grate is full of fate,
    Cups, prizes, stars—
Gold tips—generalships—
    Straight throw and kick—
Lucky Latin and easy Greek,
Holidays every mortal week,
Sober Dicky has seen them all, O sober Dick!

When coals are dark and dead,
    All burnt to dust,
Sink, light, and turn to night—
    So Fancy must!

Warm flame, vision of Fame,
Fades passing quick ;
Was the coal a teller of truth ?
Does imagining poison youth ?
Sober Dicky is dreaming now, O sober Dick !

XV

WILLOW THE KING

WILLOW the King is a monarch grand,
    Three in a row his courtiers stand;
Every day when the sun shines bright,
The doors of his palace are painted white,
And all the company bow their backs
To the King with his collar of cobbler's wax.
        So ho! so ho! may the courtiers sing,
        Honour and life to Willow the King!

Willow, King Willow, thy guard hold tight;
Trouble is coming before the night;
Hopping and galloping, short and strong,
Comes the Leathery Duke along;
And down the palaces tumble fast
When once the Leathery Duke gets past.
        So ho! &c.

'Who is this,' King Willow he swore,
'Hops like that to a gentleman's door?

'Who's afraid of a Duke like him?
'Fiddlededee!' says the monarch slim:
'What do you say, my courtiers three?'
And the courtiers all said 'Fiddlededee!'
    So ho! &c.

Willow the King stepped forward bold
Three good feet from his castle hold;
Willow the King stepped back so light,
Skirmished gay to the left and right;
But the Duke rushed by with a leap and a fling—
'Bless my soul!' says Willow the King.
    So ho! &c.

Crash the palaces, sad to see;
Crash and tumble the courtiers three!
Each one lays, in his fear and dread,
Down on the grass his respected head;
Each one kicks, as he downward goes,
Up in the air his respected toes.
    So ho! &c.

But the Leathery Duke he jumped so high,
Jumped till he almost touched the sky;
'A fig for King Willow,' he boasting said,
'Carry this gentleman off to bed!'

So they carried him off with the courtiers three,
And put him to bed in the green-baize tree.
      So ho! &c.

'What of the Duke?' you ask anon,
'Where has his Leathery Highness gone?'
O he is filled with air inside—
Either it's air, or else it's pride—
And he swells and swells as tight as a drum,
And they kick him about till Christmas come.
      So ho! ho! ho! may his courtiers sing,
      Honour and life to Willow the King!

XVI

JUNE AND THE SCHOLAR

The Scholar

What a tune,
Kind June,
You are singing all the noon,
Where the grove makes merry with the breeze, with the breeze,
Low and merry, all the song
That the wind bears along,
O June, be a sister, and stay among the trees!

June

Never fear,
Scholar dear,
In the morning of the year,
Was not all the sunny beauty made for you, made for you?
Take the bright shiny day,
Take the pleasure and the play,
The shade and the twilight, the dawning and the dew.

The Scholar

Do not fly,
Sweet sky,
Though the blaze of morning die,
Stay and linger in the flushing of the west, of the west;
If you go, they will fade,
Soft meadow, sunny glade,
The glow into dulness, the music into rest.

June

When the rose
Full blows,
When the surly winter goes,
I will come with the swallows and the sun, and the sun,
And the grass shall be bright
In the glad June light;
Far and away, till the world is dead and gone.

XVII

CATS AND DOGS

['He hath got a quiet catch.'—*Taming of the Shrew*, II. i.]

FOR cats and dogs the custom is to wrangle as they play,
But youths intent on games should be more sensible than they!
A low dispute in scenes polite would not be thought the thing,
Where bright in light, with dance and feast and bowl, dwell Court and King.

When in the yard at exercise you choose to take a part,
Converse with friends, whene'er you will, upon the batsman's art;
And if about a catch you hold an independent view,
Reflect it may perhaps be false, and shout not out it's true.

Football, methinks, if played at all, should go with voice
    demure ;
Of lines of sight the human eye can hardly e'er be sure ;
But cries proclaiming eagerly where balls have passed in
    air
Would shame a wolf, and in the dust abase a polar bear.

XVIII

FAIRIES

WHEN in the morning cold and bleak,
    In spite of wind and weather,
The wise and foolish, strong and weak,
    Throng up to School together,
From off the plain, from round the hill,
    The fairy thoughts arisen
Begin the day of work and play
    With hope, and whim, and vision:
Awake the old, suggest the new,
    Heart after heart rejoices—
Ho ho! ha ha! Tra la la la!—
    So sound the fairy voices.

From all the lowland western lea,
    The Uxbridge flats and meadows,
From where the Ruislip waters see
    The Oxhey lights and shadows;
They tell of rambles near and far,
    By hedge, and brook, and border;
Of random freak and frolic war,
    And Freedom born of Order;

Of Friendship, knit with wealth of wit,
   And wisdom linked about it—
Ho ho! ha ha! Tra la la la!—
   Or quite as close without it!

From Wembley rise and Kenton stream;
   From Preston farm and hollow,
Where Lyon dreamed, and saw in dream
   His race of sons to follow;
They point to Labour's leaden feet,
   To Glory's glow and glitter;
To sweets of Learning, partly sweet,
   And even partly bitter;
They chant in time a stately rhyme,
   The sober songs of matin—
Ho ho! ha ha! Tra la la la!—
   And quaver into Latin!

And as from north and east amain
   They throng, the fairy people,
The echoes range across the plain,
   And gather round the steeple;
Through football acres, grass and clay,
   The mighty murmurs quicken;
From goal to goal they swifter roll,
   And swell, and throb, and thicken;

Like beat of drums the music comes,
    While viewless voices mingle—
Ho ho! ha ha! Tra la la la!
    And set the veins a-tingle.

O'er twenty leagues of morning dew,
    Across the cheery breezes,
Can fairies fail to whisper true
    What youth and fancy pleases?
As strength decays with after days,
    And eyes have ceased to glisten,
Those souls alone not older grown
    Will have the ears to listen.
Keep youth a guest of heart and breast,
    And, though the hair be whiter,—
Ho ho! ha ha! Tra la la la!
    You hear them all the brighter!

XIX

JACK AND JOE

JACK'S a scholar, as all men say,
　　Dreams in Latin and Greek,
Gobbles a grammar in half a day,
　　And a lexicon once a week;
Three examiners came to Jack,
　　'Tell to us all you know;'
But when he began, 'To Oxford back,'
　　They murmured, 'we will go.'
　　　　But Joe is a regular fool, says Jack,
　　　　　　And Jack is a fool, says Joe.

Joe's a player, and no mistake,
　　Comes to it born and bred,
Dines in pads for the practice' sake,
　　Goes with a bat to bed.
Came the bowler and asked him, 'Pray,
　　Shall I bowl you fast or slow?'
But the bowler's every hair was gray
　　Before he had done with Joe.
　　　　But Joe is a regular fool, &c.

Morning wakes with a rousing spell,
    Bees and honey and hive,
Drones get up at the warning bell,
    But Jack was at work at five.
Sinks the day on the weary hill,
    Cricketers homeward flow;
All climb up in the twilight chill,
    But the last to leave is Joe.
        But Joe is a regular fool, &c.

'Fame,' says Jack, 'with the mind must go,'
    Says Joe, 'With the legs and back;'
'What is the use of your arms?' says Joe,
    'Where are your brains?' says Jack.
Says Joe, 'Your Latin I truly hate,'
    Says Jack, 'I adore it so,'
'But your bats,' says Jack, 'I nowhere rate,'
    'My darlings,' answers Joe.
        But Joe is a regular fool, &c.

Can't you settle it, Joe and Jack,
    Settle it, books and play?
Dunce is white and pedant is black,
    Haven't you room for gray?

Let neither grammar nor bats be slack,
  Let brains with sinews grow,
And you'll be Reverend Doctor Jack,
  And you'll be General Joe!
    But Joe is a regular fool, &c.

XX

WIMBLEDON, 1879

WAKE, Harrow boys, together,
    Wake, townsmen, up!
Here's the Shield, marching hither,
    Likewise the Cup.
Drums, beat to rouse the people,
    Fifes, tootle too!
Back home to Harrow steeple
    Welcome to you!
        Wake, Harrow boys, &c.

First day of summer weather,
    First ray of sun;
Twelve schools are in together,
    Odds, twelve to one.
Twelve schools are off together,
    Gone home to sup;
Left the Shield, marching hither,
    Likewise the Cup!
        Wake, Harrow boys, &c.

In came the Duke all ready,
    Plume, sash, and spurs ;
'Who's that a winning,' said he,
    ' Over the furze ?
' Why, bless my hat and feather,
    ' What can be up ?
' There's the Shield, marching thither,
    ' Likewise the Cup ! '
        Wake, Harrow boys, &c.

Bismarck and Cetewayo,
    Pale down to boots,
Ejaculate ' O my O,
    ' How Harrow shoots ! '
Once give them grass and heather,
    Once rifles up—
Straight the Shield marches hither,
    Likewise the Cup !
        Wake, Harrow boys, &c.

XXI

LARRY

WHO is Larry, and what is his sin?
    What has he done to be so discredited?
String, and leather, and air within,
    Never an ounce of brains inherited;
Up and volley him into the sky;
Down he will tumble by-and-bye;
    Flout and flurry him, kick and worry him,
Doesn't he like a journey high!

Tie up his throat, or he feels the air;
    Very unwise, to lounge and tarry is;
Give him a kick, and it sets him square,
    Kicks are physic for such as Larry is;
Over the grassy marsh and mud,
Like a bubble of soap and sud,
    Flout and flurry him, kick and worry him,
Till he is down with a thump and thud!

Little he knows, and nought he cares,
    Whether you kick with grace and suavity;
Down he will come without the stairs,
    All along of the force of gravity;
Larry is fat, and needs to go;
Larry is dull and plump and slow;
    Flout and flurry him, kick and worry him,
Wake him a bit with a touch of toe!

That is his path, where the swallows roam,
    That is a road that needs no gravelling;
Life is dull, if you bide at home;
    Larry is made of stuff for travelling!
Now you may lift him once again,
Give him a view of park and plain;
    Flout and flurry him, kick and worry him,
That is the way to induce a brain!

XXII

ROOKS

HIGH on a tree,
    Like a Pope to see,
A blackamoor rook (and as grave as he)
    Laid down the law
    With ponderous caw,
With a tweak of head and a twist of jaw,
    ' Follow the rest
    Out of the nest,
Perch on the steeple, and peck with the best!'

'Try your wing,
    Now in the spring,
Hop and flutter and fight and sing;
    Rooklings' joys
    Are worry and noise,
Soon in the air you will gladly poise,
    And '*follow the rest,*' &c.

'Branches yield
    Shelter and shield,
But the best of the fun is far afield ;
    Those who know
    Where a flight can go,
Rob the wheat that the farmers sow.
    '*Follow the rest,*' &c.

'Starlings preach,
    With twitter of speech,
How many yards a gun can reach ;
    Fly amain
    Over the plain !
Chance the gun, if you get the grain !
    '*Follow the rest,*' &c.

'Up with the head !
    Fondled, fed,
Here you may rest awhile in bed ;
    Wait for the time
    When your wings shall climb
Over the sky in the morning's prime !
    '*Follow the rest*
    Out of the nest,
Perch on the steeple, and peck with the best !'

XXIII

DOWN THE HILL

JOG, jog, tramp, tramp, down the hill we run,
   When the summer games come with the summer
      sun ;
On the grass dreaming a lazy grassy dream,
List to the merry click, willow tapping seam ;
Balls ring, throats sing, to a gallant tune,
Cheerily, cheerily, goes the afternoon.
   Down the hill, down the hill, after dinner drop,
   Sulky boys, sulky boys, stay upon the top !

Jog, jog, tramp, tramp, down the hill we scud,
In the dull December, plashing in the mud ;
Legs, as their manner is, turn to black and blue ;
Mud spatters head to foot—well, and if it do ?
Legs yet will carry us through another day ;
Mud is only water modifying clay.
   Down the hill, down the hill, after dinner drop,
   Sulky boys, sulky boys, stay upon the top !

Jog, jog, tramp, tramp, down the hill at last,
When the Tuesday morning tells of labour past;
Now, just a week or two, put the books to bed,
Horse, dog, gun and rod, you come out instead;
Who wouldn't, now and then, amiably thus
Gratify the home folks with a sight of us?
    Down the hill, down the hill, after dinner drop,
    Sulky boys, sulky boys, stay upon the top!

XXIV

AWAKE!

THE wind blew o'er the plain, and cried
    Awake, boys, awake!
The best of the day is the morning tide,
    Awake, boys, awake!
With a plunge and a rush to the air, the air,
And safe in the school, with a chime to spare,
And who, if it freeze with winter breeze,
Is half a coward enough to care?
    Or grieve if he, in his ardour bold,
    Or even his master, catches cold?
      So awake, boys, awake!
      The joys of the morning take!
They sleep in the city, and more's the pity,
    But you on the hills, awake!

The spring came whispering, clear and low,
    Awake, boys, awake!
The birds were building an hour ago,
    Awake, boys, awake!
The lark is lost in the blue, the blue,
The cricketing fields are drenched in dew;

The delicate things on feet and wings
Are busily finding work to do ;
    And every animal, great or less,
    Has dressed as much as it means to dress !
    So awake, &c.

Work, with her sister, Play, came by—
    Awake, boys, awake !
Plenty to learn from both, they cry,
    Awake, boys, awake !
There's pleasure in toil no doubt, no doubt ;
There's also pleasure, perhaps, without ;
There's books that pray to be read to-day,
There's balls that long to be kicked about ;
    But none who roost on the Drowsy tree
    Can ever be friends with me, or me !
    So awake, &c.

XXV

GOOD NIGHT

GOOD night! Ten o'clock is nearing;
   Lights from Hampstead, many, fewer, more,
Fainting, fuller, vanishing, appearing,
   Flash and float a friendly greeting o'er;
      Read them, read them,
         Ere the slumber come;
      Goodwill speed them
         Here across the gloom;
   All good comes to those who read aright;
   See they are twinkling, Good night!

Good night! How they dart anigh thee
   Bright glad rays for repetition known;
If the task be crabbed and defy thee,
   How they blink a sympathetic groan!
      Wit acuter—
         Guesses free and fast—
      Tyrant tutor
         Placable at last—
   Such the blessings sparkle to the sight;
   Take them and answer, Good night!

Good night! What shall follow after?
    Wish great play, and vigour ever new,
Wish for race and merriment and laughter—
    Hampstead lights must surely wish it too!
        Luck befriend thee
            From the very toss;
        See, they send thee
            Victory across;
Speed the ball, and animate the fight:
So, till the morning, Good night!

Good night! Sleep, and so may ever
    Lights half seen across a murky lea,
Child of hope, and courage, and endeavour,
    Gleam a voiceless benison on thee!
        Youth be bearer
            Soon of hardihood;
        Life be fairer,
            Loyaller to good;
Till the far lamps vanish into light,
Rest in the dream-time. Good night!

XXVI

SONGS

How does the song come,
   Whence up-swell,
Whence on the tongue come,
   Playmates, tell!
Say, from the waste time
   Chance sounds grow,
Throats' idle pastime?
   No, no, no!
While 'mid the breezes
   Life breathes free,
Ere trouble freezes
   Youth's blue sea,
'Mid hopes attendant,
   Play, work, home,
Surging, resplendent—
   So songs come!

Where does the song go,
   While words fly,
Somewhere along go,
   Somewhere die?
Say, into far land
   Sound-waves flow,

Lost in the star-land?
    No, no, no!
Songs, where the thought was,
    If aught true,
If tender aught was,
    There hide too;
Down in the chamber
    Hearts hold deep,
Cradled in amber—
    So songs sleep!

Can yet the song live,
    Once more come,
Voiceful and strong live—
    Now all dumb?
Say, will it slumber,
    Faint, thin, low,
Years not to number?
    No, no, no!
When droops the boldest,
    When hope flies,
When hearts are coldest,
    Dead songs rise;
Young voices sound still,
    Bright thoughts thrive,
Friends press around still—
    So songs live!

LORD'S, 1873

TELL them, Harrow has won again!
  Shout with a heart and will!
Shout till it float across the plain,
  And echo around the hill!
Four sad years of a long defeat
  Over and gone to-day;
Flash the news till the gladness greet
  Continents far away;
Say how, honour and fame at stake,
Somebody played for the old School's sake.

True as the speeding bullets go,
  Quick as the fencer's wrist,
Eton played to the fast and slow,
  Be it break, or rise, or twist;
Faint and feeble we hung the head;
  Hope in the heart sank low;
'Seventy-three, we surely said,
  Will be just like 'seventy-two:—
Then was the turn of the wizard's wand—
Somebody, somebody, bowled left-hand!

Two of us all too soon are gone—
   Hark to the Eton cheer!
One that we put our hopes upon
   Had chosen to wait a year.
Slow we counted them— run for run,—
   How many more to tie?
Loud we boasted the cut for one,
   And treasured the single bye—
Somebody! cover—or longstop—or—
Somebody's hitting about for four!

And somebody bowled them straight and strong,
   And somebody high and true,
And somebody threw to an inch along,
   Till somebody's hands were blue;
And when at the last we trembling said
   'Can anyone now be found
To keep, with valour of hand and head,
   For a hundred runs, his ground?'
Somebody—ah! he would, we knew,—
Somebody played it steady through!

To the ropes the last hit gaily went,
   As the first to the ropes had gone,
And we breathed as divers breathe, all spent,
   Who rise to the air and sun.

And ever when Harrow toils in vain,
    And the Harrow hopes are low,
May patience come to the rescue then,
    And pluck with the patience go;
And in all, and more than all, our play,
Somebody do as he did to-day!

LORD'S, 1878

THERE we sat in the circle vast,
    Hard by the tents, from noon,
And looked as the day went slowly past,
    And the runs came, all too soon;
And never, I think, in the years gone by,
    Since cricketer first went in,
Did the dying so refuse to die,
    Or the winning so hardly win.

Ladies clapped, as the fight was fought,
    And the chances went and came;
And talk sank low, till you almost thought
    You lived in the moving game.
O, good lads in the field they were,
    Laboured and ran and threw;
But we that sat on the benches there
    Had the hardest work to do!

Feet that had sped in games of yore,
    Eyes that had guarded well,
Waited and watched the mounting score,
    And the hopes that rose and fell;

And girls put frolic and wagers by,
    As they felt their pulses throb ;
And old men cheered—but the cheering cry
    Went gurgling into a sob !

What is it? forty, thirty more ?
    You in the trousers white,
What did you come to Harrow for,
    If we lose the match to-night !
If a finger's grasp, as a catch comes down,
    Go a thousandth part astray—
Heavens ! to think there are folks in town
    Who talk of the game as play !

' Over '—batsmen steadily set ;
    ' Over '—maiden again ;
If it lasts a score of overs yet,
    It may chance to turn the brain.
End it, finish it ! such a match
    Shortens the breath we draw.
Lose it at once, or else—A catch !
    Ah !

*FROM THE VISITORS' BOOK, BUTTER-
MERE INN, CRUMMOCKWATER.*

ST. GEORGE was spent—so runs the lay told still o'er pipes and flagons,—
With weeding Britain all the day of griffins, gnomes, and dragons;
Of all the sprites of hill and tree, hard hitters, merry fighters,
And almost—but that could not be—of all the guide-book writers:
Now, fighting o'er, he needed sore—oh! and his wings were weary!—
Some silent dell by fount and fell, quiet and cool and cheery:
He glanced at Malvern's boasted side, Snowdon in cloud-land hidden,
'Snowdon,' he cried, 'is cockneyfied, and Malvern physic-ridden.
The Lakes will rest the good saint best; unblessed with wife or daughter,
I yet can trace my cousin's face, St. Patrick, o'er the water.'

At Lowood's inn St. George he tried—what? with no bride beside him?—
At Ambleside he next applied—Miss Martineau defied him!
Rydal had got nor dish nor pot to welcome the newcomer,
Wast Head was full of Alpine men, in training for the summer.
At length he spied a smooth hill side, with lake and meadow planted,
Encircled all with mountain wall, deep bosomed, fairy haunted;
He looked no more—his doubt was o'er—with most angelic flutter
His pinions drooped, and down he swooped, down, on the Mere of Butter.
The matron gave what matrons have of welcome and of dinner,
What best they give to all who crave, be they or saint or sinner.
She gave him eggs—she broiled him ham—she would have added nectar,
But who can think what saints may drink?—unless indeed the rector.
'Woman,' St. George at parting said, 'thy whisky's not the poorest;

Thy chops are good for heavenly food, and any mortal tourist.
Be thou the patron of the vale, of cot and farm and dairy,
The queen of inns o'er hill and dale, of hostels tutelary;
And when the guest comes sore distressed from Pillar, Scarf, or Gable,
With thee he best shall find good rest, good bed and eke good table;
Nor when he begs with weary legs, feet sore, and empty stomach,
Shall see or hear of better cheer than by the Lake of Crummock.'

AN EPISODE OF BALACLAVA

WHEN slow and faint from off the plain
    Pale wrecks of sword and gun,
Torn limbs, and faces racked with pain,
    Crept upwards, one by one;
When, striving as the hopeless strive,
    Ascare with shot and flame,
Few pallid riders came alive,
    And marvelled as they came,

Dared any, while with corpses rife
    Red gleamed the ghastly track,
Ride, for the love of more than life,
    Into the valley back?
Pierce, where the bravest tarried not,
    Stand, where the strongest fell,
Face once again the surge of shot,
    The plunging hail of shell?

He trod of old the hill we tread,
    He played the games we play;
The part of him that is not dead
    Belongs to us to-day;

When next the stranger scans the wall
    Where carved our heroes are,
Wits—poets—statesmen—shew them all,
    And then, the one hussar.

He sought his chief—a dim reply
    From waving hand was brought ;
' Passed on '—*to safety*, meant the cry ;
    Amid the guns, he thought ;
No question more ; in purpose clear
    His soldier's creed was strong ;
Where rode, he knew, the brigadier,
    Must ride the aide-de-camp !

He turned his horse's bridle round,
    Ere one could breathe a breath,
And fronted, as on practice ground,
    The nearest way to death.
In pride of manhood's ripest spring,
    Hopes high, and honour won,
He deemed his life a little thing,
    And rode, a soldier, on.

Up, slow, the homeward remnant fled,
    Staggered, and fell, and ran ;
Down moved, through flying and through dead,
    One hopeless splendid man ;

Alone, unrecked in heat of fray,
   He stemmed the wave of flight,
And passed in smoke and flame away
   From safety and from sight.

So ends the story ; comrade none
   Saw where he wounded lay ;
No brother helped with cheering tone
   His stricken life away ;
Alone, the pain, the chill, the dread,
   Crept on him, limb by limb ;
The earth which hides the nameless dead
   Closed nameless over him.

O soldiers of a bloodless strife,
   O friends in work and play,
Bear we not all a coward life
   Some moment in the day ?
So, lest a deed of gallant faith
   Forgotten fade from view,
I take the tale of LOCKWOOD's death,
   And write it down for you.

P. L. C.

NOT surely a week since we saw him,
    Health brimming in feature and limb;
Let me try to imagine and draw him,
    Ere fancy and feature are dim.
Tall, eager, a face to remember,
    A flush that could change as the day;
A spirit that knew not December,
    That brightened the sunshine of May.

A child; in his childhood contented;
    Soon clouded, and sooner serene;
Faults many, and quickly repented;
    Much love, where repentance had been.
Strong life, and an ardour of living;
    Quick blood, to enjoy and to hope;
Most happy when, void of misgiving,
    He coloured the world to his scope.

Is gentleness dear to the sainted?
    Is simpleness precious above?
Shall a soul, with humanity tainted,
    Through humbleness quicken to love?

O comrades, when, in him and through him,
    As weakness and brightness would blend,
You saw the soft nature, and knew him,
    What more will you wish for your friend?

What is he? No answer. Behind him
    Press faces as gallant as he.
Perchance you may happen to find him
    As you roam through the ages to be.
There will still be the smile, and more golden;
    There will still be the trust, and more true;
And, with manhood to nerve and embolden,
    The boy will be dearer to you.

1873.

SHEMUEL

SHEMUEL, the Bethlehemite,
  Watched a fevered guest at night;
All his fellows fared afield,
Saw the angel host revealed;
He nor caught the mystic story,
Heard the song, nor saw the glory.

Through the night they gazing stood,
Heard the holy multitude;
Back they came in wonder home,
Knew the Christmas kingdom come,
Eyes aflame, and hearts elated;
Shemuel sat alone, and waited.

Works of mercy now, as then,
Hide the angel host from men;
Hearts atune to earthly love
Miss the angel notes above;
Deeds, at which the world rejoices,
Quench the sound of angel voices.

So they thought, nor deemed from whence
His celestial recompense.
Shemuel, by the fever bed,
Touched by beckoning hands that led,
Died, and saw the Uncreated ;
All his fellows lived, and waited.

R. G.

STILL the balls ring upon the sun-lit grass,
    Still the big elms, deep shadowed, watch the play;
And ordered game and loyal conflict pass
    The hours of May.

But the game's guardian, mute, nor heeding more
    What suns may gladden, and what airs may blow,
Friend, teacher, playmate, helper, counsellor,
    Lies resting now.

'Over'—they move, as bids their fieldsman's art;
    With shifted scene the strife begins anew;
'Over'—we seem to hear him, but his part
    Is over, too.

Dull the best speed, and vain the surest grace—
    So seemed it ever—till there moved along
Brimmed hat, and cheering presence, and tried face
    Amid the throng.

He swayed his realm of grass, and planned, and wrought;
   Warned rash intruders from the tended sward;
A workman, deeming, for the friends he taught,
   No service hard.

He found, behind first failure, more success;
   Cheered stout endeavour more than languid skill;
And ruled the heart of boyhood with the stress
   Of helpful will.

Or, standing at our hard-fought game, would look,
   Silent and patient, drowned in hope and fear,
Till the lips quivered, and the strong voice shook
   With low glad cheer.

Well played. His life was honester than ours;
   We scheme, he worked, we hesitate, he spoke;
His rough-hewn stem held no concealing flowers,
   But grain of oak.

No earthly umpire speaks, his grave above;
   And thanks are dumb, and praise is all too late;
That worth and truth, that manhood and that love
   Are hid, and wait.

Sleep gently, where thou sleepest, dear old friend ;
   Think, if thou thinkest, on the bright days past ;
Yet loftier Love, and worthier Truth attend
   What more thou hast !

1884.

www.ingramcontent.com/pod-product-compliance
Lightning Source LLC
Chambersburg PA
CBHW031605110426
42742CB00037B/1221